Set design by Robert Brill

Photo by T. Charles Erickson

The set of the Long Wharf Theatre production of *The Story*.

THE STORY

BY TRACEY SCOTT WILSON

★

★

DRAMATISTS
PLAY SERVICE
INC.

THE STORY premiered at the Joseph Papp Public Theater/New York Shakespeare Festival (George C. Wolfe, Producer; Mara Manus, Executive Director; Michael Hurst, Managing Director) in New York City, opening on December 10, 2003. It was directed by Loretta Greco; the set design was by Robert Brill; the lighting design was by James Vermeulen; the original music and sound design were by Robert Kaplowitz; the costume design was by Emilio Sosa; the production stage manager was Buzz Cohen; and the stage manager was Damon W. Arrington. The cast was as follows:

YVONNE	Erika Alexander
ASSISTANT/ENSEMBLE	Kalimi A. Baxter
LATISHA	Tammi Clayton
NEIL	Damon Gupton
DETECTIVE/ENSEMBLE	Michelle Hurst
JEFF/TIM DUNN	Stephen Kunken
PAT	Phylicia Rashad
REPORTER/ENSEMBLE	Susan Kelechi Watson
JESSICA DUNN	Sarah Grace Wilson

THE STORY was subsequently produced by the Long Wharf Theatre (Gordon Edelstein, Artistic Director; Michael Stotts, Managing Director) in New Haven, Connecticut, opening on February 11, 2004. It was directed by Loretta Greco; the set design was by Robert Brill; the lighting design was by James Vermeulen; the original music and sound design were by Robert Kaplowitz; the costume design was by Emilio Sosa; and the production stage manager was Buzz Cohen. The cast was as follows:

YVONNE	Lizzy Cooper Davis
ASSISTANT/ENSEMBLE	Kalimi A. Baxter
LATISHA	Tammi Clayton
NEIL	Duane Boutté
DETECTIVE/ENSEMBLE	Michelle Hurst
JEFF/TIM DUNN	David Wilson Barnes
PAT	Sharon Washington
REPORTER/ENSEMBLE	Christen Simon
JESSICA DUNN	Sarah Grace Wilson

CHARACTERS

YVONNE

ASSISTANT/ENSEMBLE

LATISHA

NEIL

DETECTIVE/ENSEMBLE

JEFF/TIM DUNN

PAT

REPORTER/ENSEMBLE

JESSICA DUNN

PLACE

An American city.

TIME

The present.

THE STORY

ACT ONE

Prologue

DETECTIVE. Please state your full name.

JESSICA. Jessica Alisha Dunn.

DETECTIVE. Your address.

JESSICA. 4600 Sycamore Ave, Glenridge.

DETECTIVE. At approximately eight P.M. were you and your husband driving in the Northside area?

JESSICA. Yes.

DETECTIVE. Your husband was driving the car?

JESSICA. Yes. *(Lights up on Tim, her husband.)*

TIM. Where are we?

JESSICA. I don't know.

TIM. What does the paper say?

JESSICA. The paper says the address. It doesn't say where we are.

TIM. Just let me see it.

JESSICA. No, it won't do any good. You don't know where we are.

TIM. Let me see it. *(She doesn't. Continuing; looking out window.)* I'll ask that guy over there. *(Lights up on a black person in hooded jacket, street clothes.)*

JESSICA. No, don't ask anybody in this neighborhood.

TIM. Stop being so racist. What is wrong with you?

JESSICA. Nothing is wrong with me. Do you see where we are?

TIM. Of course, I see where we are. We go to work here every day, don't we?

DETECTIVE. You and your husband are ... were teachers.

JESSICA. Yes, in the Teach America program.

DETECTIVE. You taught at Benjamin Banneker?

JESSICA. Yes, just a few blocks from where ... *(She cries. Detective*

gives her tissues.)
DETECTIVE. Would you like …
JESSICA. No, no let's just … *(To Tim.)* It's not so scary in the daytime. This is night. Very dark night. Let's just go home.
TIM. No. Mom and Dad are probably there already.
JESSICA. Too bad. They'll understand. This is scary.
TIM. If you act terrified, how are we ever supposed to convince Mom and Dad that what we're doing is a good idea? Huh? This was your idea. Dinner in the neighborhood so they can see.
JESSICA. That was before … now … I want to go home. I want to go home.
TIM. That looks like a ramp.
JESSICA. It does not. *(Pause.)* Tim, I'm really scared.
TIM. Honey, don't be scared. We know this neighborhood.
JESSICA. We don't. How are we going to get back? *(Jessica cries.)*
DETECTIVE. Would you like a glass of water?
JESSICA. No, no. I'm alright. I'm alright. There was a gas station. *(To Detective.)* It looked sort of shady, but there were a lot of people around. There was this black gentleman getting gas. *(Lights up on black man in a nice suit. Continuing.)* He had a suit on. He looked … conservative.
DETECTIVE. Did you get his name?
JESSICA. No.
DETECTIVE. Do you remember his car?
JESSICA. A BMW or Lexus. It was a nice car. Not flashy. He was playing classical music on his car radio. *(Classical music plays. Continuing.)* Which surprised me. And there was a woman in the car. She was dressed nice too. *(Lights up on a nicely dressed black woman.)*
DETECTIVE. A black woman?
JESSICA. Yes. She was wearing a red dress.
DETECTIVE. A red dress?
JESSICA. Yeah. It was red. I remember that. Red is my favorite color.
DETECTIVE. Did she speak to you?
JESSICA. No, she smiled. *(Woman smiles. Jessica smiles back. Continuing.)* I remember that. She smiled at me and she seemed nice.
DETECTIVE. The black gentleman gave you directions.
JESSICA. Yeah … but … I … *(To Tim.)* We're lost again.
TIM. We're not.
JESSICA. We are. He said turn right two blocks back. Tim, we're lost. We are los … *(Jessica screams.)* TIM! *(Sound of two gunshots. Then lights up on a television reporter reading from copy.)*

REPORTER. "He didn't have to teach. His father, Alex Dunn, a self-made billionaire, told him so. But he did. And last night he wanted to prove to his parents that he was right to do so. So at seven P.M., Tim Dunn and his wife into got their 1990 Honda Accord and drove downtown to meet their parents at Alcove, a trendy new Brazilian restaurant located in an area that has been abandoned and neglected since the 1960's."

JESSICA. I was frozen. Just frozen. He said ...

DETECTIVE. Who said?

JESSICA. He said ...

TIM. Please don't! Please don't! We're having a baby! *(Jessica starts crying.)*

JESSICA. Please, please. Let this be all. *(Pause.)* Let this be all.

DETECTIVE. OK ... *(Pause.)* OK ...

REPORTER. "They wanted to show their parents the area had changed. They wanted to show their parents it wasn't so dangerous. They wanted to show their parents they were right to turn down lucrative jobs in the private sector to teach poor inner city students with monumental problems. They wanted to help." *(Police siren and lights. We see black males handcuffed, hands behind backs, assuming the position.)*

Scene 1

Lights up on a newsroom. Jeff, a white man in his mid-twenties, and Yvonne, a black woman in her mid-twenties, enter. There are two distinct areas, the Metro area and Outlook area. Also there should be an "outside area" that signifies the outside world, people's homes, etc. There should be no blackouts between scenes and the play should move as quickly as possible.

JEFF. And, finally, I think your desk will probably be over there somewhere.

YVONNE. That's the Outlook section ... way over there?

JEFF. Yeah, over there. From the wall to that desk.

YVONNE. Small section. Much smaller than Metro, I see.

JEFF. Just as important.

YVONNE. Come on.

JEFF. No, no. It is. Outlook's become the hot section. People are taking it seriously now. With the Dunn murder everyone's looking at it for … perspective.

YVONNE. I don't have any perspective on murders committed by black people.

JEFF. We don't know the murder was committed by a black person.

YVONNE. In that neighborhood? Come on now. *(Jeff tries to interrupt. Continuing.)* Alright, alright. It doesn't matter. Like I told you earlier honey, I don't plan on being at Ebony/Jet Junior for long. Soon, I'll be at Metro with you, then onto the National desk, then … *(Notices Jeff's expression.)* What?

JEFF. First, we can't be so familiar. We have to be professional.

YVONNE. Really? I can't have sex with you in the copy room during lunch? Damn, I asked them that during my interview. They said it'd be alright.

JEFF. Come on now listen, I told you how things are around here. We just … We can't slip up and say honey or baby or anything like that around other people. *(Pause.)* Especially Neil.

YVONNE. Yes, baby, honey, sweetheart, love of my life. Can I call you Jeff or do you want me to call you Mr. Morgan?

JEFF. And you have to be careful with that Ebony/Jet Junior stuff. People don't like that.

YVONNE. People like who? Neil? What's wrong with Neil?

JEFF. Nothing, but I think … *(Jeff looks around, making sure they are alone. Continuing.)* One time his sister was dating a white guy and I heard, overheard, he didn't like it very much.

YVONNE. Oh, come on. Is that why we can't be too familiar? Is he going to sick da brothers on us?

JEFF. Yvonne, listen. I don't want people in our business. I'm telling you. Racial politics are very tenuous here. Very. Everybody's edgy. And I think it would be good if you … You know, Neil and your boss are very close. He's like second in command over there.

YVONNE. So Pat doesn't like white folks either? She didn't even stay for the rest of my interview. Very tacky. Very unprofessional.

JEFF. She was on deadline.

YVONNE. No, she's …

JEFF. I'm just saying. Things are very tenuous. Very.

YVONNE. That Pat reminds me of my cousin Adrienne. Adrienne would come over to my house, pull on my hair and ask me why I always acted so white. So, I asked my daddy why I acted so white and he told me I wasn't acting white, Adrienne just acted like a nigger.

JEFF. OK ... OK ... That's a good example right there. Don't ever tell that story to anybody around here ... ever. OK? Yvonne. I'm serious. Ever.

YVONNE. If Chris Rock said that you'd be rolling on the floor right now. *(Jeff starts to interrupt. Continuing; pause.)* Forget it. Let's just go to dinner. Don't worry about Pat and Neil either. I'll be down with them. I be's more black. I be from the streets. *(Rapping.)*

My name is Yvonne

My game is always on

A reporter from the hood

I really think I should

Up to no good. *(Jeff kisses Yvonne. Then he suddenly stops, and looks around nervously. Continuing.)* What? What's wrong?

JEFF. I thought I saw somebody.

Scene 2

Next day. Neil, a black man in his mid-twenties, and Pat, a black woman in her early forties, enter. Jeff is not there.

PAT. You've come at an exciting time. It's crazy, busy. We're redesigning, adding new features.

YVONNE. I thought my desk would be over there somewhere. Isn't the Outlook section over there?

PAT. Most of us are over there but we've run out of desk space so ... We'll just put you over here for now.

YVONNE. This will be fine, thank you.

PAT. OK ... Well, I don't know how much they told you about how we work around here. Again, I apologize for leaving in the middle of your interview but ...

YVONNE. No ... no ... that's fine. I understand. You know I've worked for several papers. I'm familiar with the workings ...

PAT. We work a little different. Outlook works a little different. Listen, if I didn't have to leave that day I would have told you how things are around here for us. I'm sure you've noticed that we are in short supply. For years they tried to stick us in one place. The Metro desk.

NEIL. Every day, the Metro desk would have a picture of some brother doing the perp walk. Every day.

PAT. Then one day ... Sorry for interrupting, Neil. Then one day ...

NEIL. About six years ago.

PAT. About six years ago.

NEIL. Somebody got the pictures confused.

PAT. They used a picture of a brother that was taken two years earlier.

NEIL. But nobody noticed because it was just another brother doing the perp walk.

PAT. That's how it was but we complained and cajoled.

NEIL. Pat complained and cajoled.

PAT. And we got Outlook.

NEIL. In the past year alone, we exposed corruption and discrimination in public housing ...

PAT. And the DMV.

NEIL. And the DMV. But I've never seen anything like this. This murder has got all the white folks up in arms.

PAT. Yes. It's crazy. My son was stopped twice yesterday. I went ballistic. *(To Yvonne.)* Did you read my column this morning?

YVONNE. No.

PAT. Oh, well, I wrote about it.

YVONNE. I was in such a rush this morning ...

NEIL. It was a great piece. *(Awkward pause.)*

PAT. Thank you. *(Awkward pause again.)*

NEIL. *(Continuing.)* They stopped me this morning.

PAT. Did they?

NEIL. A random police check of cars, but you know who they were looking for.

PAT. Uh-huh. They don't bother checking out Miss Dunn though.

NEIL. No, of course not. Of course not.

PAT. *(To Neil.)* How's your piece going?

NEIL. Oh, great, great. Some very interesting developments. Very interesting.

PAT. *(To Yvonne.)* Neil has been checking out the grieving widow.

NEIL. Yeah, you know when a spouse is murdered, the other spouse is always, always a prime suspect.

PAT. Uh-huh. Except when the spouse is white and screams, "A BIG, BLACK MAN DID IT! A BIG, BLACK MAN DID IT!"

(Pat and Neil crack up laughing. Yvonne is not amused at all.)
NEIL. You got that right. *(More laughter. Pause. Yvonne still does not respond. Pat's cell phone rings.)*
PAT. Damn … I'm sorry. *(Checks phone.)* I have to take this. Please excuse me. Neil, will you take over? Just, you know, give her the 411.
NEIL. Alright. No problem. No problem. *(Pat leaves. Continuing.)* So … You really impressed everybody in your interview. Harvard. *Summa cum laud.* Sorbonne. Two, no, four languages right?
YVONNE. I learned several languages early on. *(Lights up on Jeff. Continuing; to Jeff.)* He was hitting on me.
NEIL. *(To Yvonne.)* Oh, yes. *Oui, c'est très simple quand vous êtes jeune.* *
YVONNE. And showing off.
NEIL. You know, I almost went to Harvard.
YVONNE. *(To Jeff.)* First day, I could not believe it. *(To Neil.)* Did you? *(Lights up on Pat.)*
NEIL. *(To Yvonne.)* Told them I was going and everything. *(To Pat.)* She one of them uncertain sisters. *(To Yvonne.)* But at the last minute, I changed my mind. *(To Pat.)* Uncertain to the core. *(To Yvonne.)* I went to Howard instead.
JEFF. *(To Yvonne.)* Maybe you read him wrong.
PAT. *(To Neil.)* Uncertain sister?
JEFF. *(To Yvonne.)* Maybe he was just being friendly.
PAT. *(To Neil.)* What's that?
YVONNE. *(To Jeff.)* I know when a guy is hitting on me. *(To Neil.)* Howard's in Washington right? *(To Jeff.)* His eyes checking me out.
NEIL. *(To Yvonne.)* Right. *(To Pat.)* You see, uncertain sisters … *(To Yvonne.)* Harvard seemed too much like Andover. *(To Pat.)* Are always on the defensive. *(To Yvonne.)* I wanted to have experiences I was denied.
YVONNE. *(To Neil.)* You went to boarding school? *(To Jeff.)* Telling me all that personal stuff. *(To Neil.)* I went to Groton. *(To Jeff.)* We just met. *(To Neil.)* Did you like it? *(To Jeff.)* Black men always …
NEIL. *(To Yvonne.)* Well, great education. *(To Pat.)* That's what we would call them in college. *(To Yvonne.)* But I left Andover hungry for the black experience. *(To Pat.)* Uncertain sisters. *(To Yvonne.)* Did you like … Groton did you say?
YVONNE. I loved it.

* *Yes, it's very simple when you are young.*

NEIL. *(To Pat.)* 'Cause they were uncertain about who they were. Uncertain about their place in the world, and uncertain about why they didn't return your phone calls.

YVONNE. *(To Jeff.)* I just keep telling myself. In a few months I'll transfer. In a few months I'll transfer.

JEFF. I think you have to give it a chance. It's been less than forty-eight hours.

YVONNE. It's like grammar school all over again and all the cool black kids hate me. Something in my walk. Something in my talk tells them I'm not "down." I'm not keeping it real. But this is it. This is my real.

JEFF. Just give them a chance. If Neil was hitting on you at least he likes some part of you.

YVONNE. *(To Jeff.)* He cooled down quickly. *(To Neil.)* Listen, I'd really like to get started so ... if we could ... we'll talk later?

NEIL. Oh, sure ... sure. You want to go to lunch. Some of us ...

YVONNE. I have a lunch date, but I'll call you. *(Pause.)* I'll call you.

NEIL. Oh. OK. Cool. Cool. No problem. No problem.

JEFF. Did you tell him the lunch date was with me?

YVONNE. Yes, and that we were having lunch in a hotel room naked.

JEFF. Tenuous, Yvonne. Very, very tenuous.

YVONNE. I saw Pat later. *(Pause.)* She mentioned you.

NEIL. *(To Pat.)* Did she mention me?

JEFF. Me?

PAT. *(To Neil.)* Yes. *(To Yvonne.)* Listen, what I was trying to say before we were interrupted ... I don't know what they told you in the interview but ...

YVONNE. They told me I would start here, but then I would have the opportunity to move on.

PAT. Move on to what? What goals have you set for yourself?

YVONNE. Where do I see myself in five years? I ...

PAT. Listen, they only really started hiring us six years ago. I been here for ten years. For my first four years I was the only one. *(Pause.)* The only one.

YVONNE. So do all the black reporters work at Outlook?

PAT. No, but a lot of us are there because Outlook gives us a chance to write about the positive things that are happening in our community.

YVONNE. That's very admirable, but I would like to be thought of as a reporter, not a black reporter.

PAT. Well, we all would, but that's not the reality. *(Yvonne tries to interrupt. Continuing.)* The reality is we are at a paper that has only one black editor, way behind every other major paper in the country. And the reality is this paper was notoriously racist in its portrayal of minorities and the reality is we are fighting to keep a balance in the paper every day. Every day is a battle. Every single day. Listen, where are you from originally?

YVONNE. Boston. Originally.

PAT. Boston. Uh-huh. Home of Charles Stuart.

YVONNE. Who?

PAT. Charles Stuart, the white guy who shot his pregnant wife and tried to blame it on a brother. A couple of my cousins were arrested in that raid.

YVONNE. Oh, that was ... years ago. The eighties.

PAT. Uh-huh. And the Dunn murder was only last week.

YVONNE. But that's not ... I mean ... You don't really think that's the same type of situation do you? I mean they ... the Dunns were teachers in the community. They were trying to help the community. *(Pat looks at her incredulously.)* Boston is not that bad ... My family ...

PAT. *(To Yvonne.)* Boston is Mississippi 1963.

YVONNE. *(To Pat.)* I ...

PAT. *(To Yvonne.)* Boston is Mississippi 1963 and this paper is Alabama. Understand?

YVONNE. No, I'm sorry. I really don't understand how it could be that bad here. How ...

PAT. Your generation just doesn't grasp the sacrifices made on your behalf and ...

YVONNE. *(To Jeff.)* God, if I had a dollar for every time an old black person said that to me ... *(To Pat.)* Uh-huh.

PAT. And it's true. A lot more doors are open, but we still have to be twice as good, twice as smart, and twice as strong to go through them. Especially here.

YVONNE. You sound like my father. An A wasn't good enough for him. He wanted to know why it wasn't an A+.

PAT. Yes, my father was the same way. When I was growing up we lived next door to this cardiologist, Dr. Summit. Dr. Summit treated white patients. It was amazing to see whites coming into our neighborhood. I think they were mostly white trash, but still, in those days ... Anyway, Summit was admired by everybody, but he wanted none of our pride. Black pride. He wouldn't accept it.

He thought of himself as an exception to the black race instead of part of it. He sent his children off to private schools. They weren't allowed to speak or play with us when they came home. Everyone else in the neighborhood was a part of Jack and Jill. You know Jack and Jill?

YVONNE. I've heard of it.

PAT. Jack and Jill where the black elite meet, but, as I said, Dr. Summit didn't want his family thinking of themselves as black.

YVONNE. Until … *(Pause. Pat looks at her.)*

PAT. Until … one of Dr. Summit's white patients died. There was an inquiry. He lost his license, his practice, everything.

YVONNE. Sad.

PAT. Yes. Some people in the neighborhood were overjoyed that he got his due, but my father wouldn't hear of it. He helped Dr. Summit get back on his feet. Now Summit owns a very successful medical supply company and he and my father are best friends.

YVONNE. Oh. *(Pause.)* Not sad then.

PAT. No. Not sad at all. *(Pause.)* Summit learned, and you will too, that, in the end, when it all hits the fan, community is all you have. That's what Outlook is about. Community.

JEFF and NEIL. What about me, though? What'd she say about …

YVONNE and PAT. She said …

PAT. *(To Yvonne.)* And the reality is the most loved person at the Metro desk is a white, Ivy League trust fund baby who knows nothing about us and is not for us.

JEFF. She said that?

YVONNE. *(To Pat.)* I sense some tension between us. Is it because of Neil? I know you two are close. I didn't mean to be short with him. I am a team player. There is no need for him to be intimidated by me. I hope to have lunch with him soon. *(Pause.)* Sometime soon.

JEFF and NEIL. She really said that?

YVONNE and PAT. *(Pause.)* Yes.

Scene 3

Lights up on Jessica Dunn. She is in a spotlight answering reporters' questions. We don't see the reporters, but we hear loud, anonymous questions.

JESSICA. No, I don't ... Three months tomorrow ... No, no it was a wonderful experience. Until ... I don't know. It was hard sometimes. Please ... I ... No, we had a good marriage, a great marri ... Who said? What? Lawsuit? Who would I sue? For what? Who has money around there? I don't know. I'm sorry about the arrest ... Those false arrests. But he was black ... I'm sure. A black male. He was ... I can't help that ... I won't ... NO! NO! NO! I won't be giving any more interviews. Please don't bother my parents. No more ... No more ... No more ... *(Lights up on Detective. During the following, Detective and Jessica only speak to each other. Neil only speaks to Jessica.)* You have to stop them from bothering me.

DETECTIVE. OK. OK. Just ...

JESSICA. No, no. I have rights. I have rights. I'm not a suspect here. I'm not a suspect. They just keep ...

NEIL. Neil Patterson, *The Daily.*

JESSICA. They distort the facts.

NEIL. Your husband was heir to an oil fortune, but you grew up very poor, correct?

JESSICA. And twist everything.

NEIL. Sources have told me you wanted to quit teaching, your husband did not. Is that correct?

JESSICA. I'm sick of it. It's making me sick.

DETECTIVE. I just ... I'm sorry. I can't control the press.

JESSICA. They don't understand.

NEIL. Why would you go to dinner in such a dangerous neighborhood without getting accurate directions?

JESSICA. They don't try to understand.

NEIL. How could you get lost six blocks ... six blocks from your job?

DETECTIVE. Maybe you should hire a lawyer.

NEIL. And is it also true that you and your husband separated a month before the murder?

JESSICA. Then everybody will think …

NEIL. Didn't your husband take out a life insurance policy one month before …

DETECTIVE. Think what?

NEIL. Don't you stand to inherit a considerable amount of money now?

DETECTIVE. Think what?

Scene 4

Pat hands Yvonne a memo after each of the following lines.

PAT. There's a community center opening up. I want you to cover that.

YVONNE. *(To Jeff.)* I'm dying inside. Just dying.

JEFF. Every reporter goes through a rough time at first. You know that.

PAT. There's a new after-school program at the Southside Community Center. Look into it.

YVONNE. *(To Jeff.)* I had four drinks at lunch today. Cosmopolitans.

JEFF. That's not good. That's not good at all.

PAT. The Eastside Community Center is celebrating their tenth anniversary. Be there by two.

YVONNE. *(To Jeff.)* If I don't get transferred soon … Death or alcoholism. Those are the options. Death … Alcoholism. Death by alcoholism.

JEFF. Just …

YVONNE. There are better stories out there. This is not what I signed up for. They're driving me crazy. *(Lights up on Pat.)*

PAT. *(To Yvonne.)* The Northside Community Center just hired a new director. Interview her.

YVONNE. *(To Jeff.)* You know how many community centers I been to? I never went to a community center once before I got this job. Not once. There was one down the street from us. My father wouldn't let us near it. Now I know why. They're all the same. Every one of them. *(Lights up on chorus women in spotlights. Each woman should have similar mannerisms.)*

LIGHT ONE. We hope to create an environment where our children can feel safe and ...

LIGHT TWO. ... They can see the positive brothers and sisters who work in the community because ...

LIGHT THREE. Our families need help and we're the only ones giving it to them. Recent government cutbacks have ...

YVONNE. Every one the same. The same. These pristine brick and stone structures located near liquor stores, ninety-nine-cent shops and churches. Inside, it's like a hospital because you get the feeling that there are all these rules and things are going on that you'll never really understand. And the community center director. Always black. Always female. Always.

LIGHT ONE. Eloise Brown.

LIGHT TWO. Ellen Turner.

LIGHT THREE. Jacquelyn Joseph.

YVONNE. Sometimes attractive. Sometimes not. Sometimes stylishly dressed. Sometimes not. But always, always, always ... A look on their faces as if they've seen the war. Up close. And they carry the wounds around in their bodies. All the time. *(Pause.)* All the time. And the students. *(Chorus women turn into teenage girls.)* Not children. Not close to it. The only thing young about them is their faces. Perfect baby skin. Smooth, unblemished cocoa-colored perfection. But underneath ... they've not only seen the war, they're in it. But they're too scared to be sad. So they just act amused. And what's worse, every time I bring a story back, Pat edits it to death. She says it's not positive enough.

PAT. *(To Yvonne.)* Are you sure about your sources here?

JEFF. *(To Yvonne.)* She says that? Not positive enough?

YVONNE. *(To Pat and Jeff.)* Yes.

PAT. *(To Yvonne.)* Because according to my research. *(To Neil.)* Her work is sloppy. *(To Yvonne.)* This center was open two years ago, not four. *(To Neil.)* Very, very sloppy. *(To Yvonne.)* They've had three directors in the past year. Not two. And they actually had an eight percent increase in federal funds. Not a decrease.

JEFF. *(To Yvonne.)*	NEIL. *(To Pat.)*
What do you say?	How does sister girl respond?
YVONNE. *(To Jeff.)*	PAT. *(To Neil.)*
What can I say?	What can she say?

YVONNE. *(To Jeff.)* I take the story back and put in a lot of "positive" adjectives. Strong black men, blah, blah, blah. Asset to the community, blah, blah, blah. Strong black women, blah, blah, blah.

PAT. *(To Neil.)* She types in my corrections like a secretary.

JEFF. *(To Yvonne.)* You don't debate?

NEIL. She doesn't put up a fight?

YVONNE. I tried to fight … once …

PAT. This one time though … She tried to say something when I told her … *(To Yvonne.)* Your writing is very biased.

YVONNE. Biased how?

PAT. You editorialize. I've noticed it creeping into a lot of your news stories.

YVONNE. Editorialize which stories? The one about community center number three? Or community center number seven.

PAT. You've written more stories than that. *(Yvonne tries to speak. Continuing.)* That profile of Congresswoman Watts … *(Pat looks for story. Finds it.)* You wrote … You wrote … um … "Congresswoman Watts came into the room smartly dressed but disoriented. Although she didn't want to comment on the recent Senate investigation against her, clearly it was on her mind." How do you know that?

YVONNE. I could tell.

PAT. Did you ask her?

YVONNE. She refused to comment.

PAT. Well, you should put it like that. This makes her seem … suspect.

YVONNE. But she is under suspicion.

PAT. So are half a dozen other congressmen.

YVONNE. I wasn't writing about half a dozen other congressmen. I was writing about her. A black female. That's the real issue right? You know what? Whatever. *(To Jeff.)* I realized there's just no point. I'll transfer soon.

JEFF. Yvonne …

PAT. *(To Neil.)* No way is she going to make it.

YVONNE. No, Jeff, I stumbled across a story today. The story.

PAT. *(To Neil.)* Despite her scoop.

JEFF. *(To Yvonne.)* What?

NEIL. *(To Pat.)* Scoop? *(Lights up on Latisha, a seventeen-year-old black girl.)*

YVONNE. *(To Jeff.)* Another assignment about a community center. Another one. As soon as I got there I decided I was going to quit. Just sit at home until a position in Metro or National opened up, but then … I saw this girl. *(To Pat.)* This girl was different.

PAT. *(To Yvonne.)* Uh-huh. Go ahead.

NEIL. *(To Pat.)* What's so different about her?

YVONNE. *(To Pat and Jeff.)*	PAT. *(To Neil.)*
You're not going to	You're not going to
believe this.	believe this.
JEFF.	NEIL *(To Pat.)*
What?	What is it?

YVONNE. *(To Jeff.)* She's in da hood, but not of it. *(To Pat.)* She was different from the girls I usually meet. A very high IQ. I'm sure.

LATISHA. *(During this scene she only speaks to Yvonne.)* My parents were activists from the sixties.

YVONNE. *(To Pat and Jeff.)* She was witty, ironic, smarter than her years.

LATISHA. Hence the pseudo-African name. *(Pointing to herself.)* Latisha.

YVONNE. *(To Pat and Jeff.)* I liked her right away.

LATISHA. The "revolution" ate them alive. My daddy became an alcoholic. My mother was one for a while too, but she recovered ... from that.

NEIL. *(To Pat.)* So?

PAT. *(To Yvonne.)* What's so remarkable ...

JEFF. ... about that?

YVONNE. *(To Pat and Jeff.)* No, no ... but listen. She's a straight-A student.

JEFF. *(To Yvonne.)* Yes, but ... That's not that hard to do in that neighborhood is it? *(Yvonne gives Jeff a look.)* You know what I mean ... *(Pause.)* I shouldn't have said that.

YVONNE. She speaks perfect Italian. We conversed for several minutes. *(To Latisha.)* Quando avete imparato italiano?

LATISHA. *Circa un anno fa. È una lingua bella.*

YVONNE. *Sì, certamente.*

LATISHA. *Spero di andare in Italia un giorno.* *

YVONNE. She taught herself.

LATISHA. I get bored, so I just read stuff. The only thing my dad ever gave me was books. Tons and tons of books, so I read and read and read and read. Whatever I can, you know.

YVONNE. That and German too.

---

* When did you learn Italian?
Around one year ago. It is a beautiful language.
Yes, certainly.
I hope to go to Italy one day.

LATISHA. *Deutsch ist sehr musikalisch.*

YVONNE. *Rufen Sie mich an, wenn Sie überhaupt üben möchten.*

LATISHA. *Danke, ich werde.* *

YVONNE. *(To Pat and Jeff.)* So we're talking, and talking, and talking.

LATISHA. I don't tell anybody around here, of course. Nobody in school either. Not even my teachers. They would make a big deal and single me out. I just want to do my time and get out. No trouble.

YVONNE. *(To Latisha.)* You shouldn't be ashamed of being smart.

LATISHA. Yeah ... I ...

YVONNE. I mean, ever. Those idiots ...

LATISHA. Idiots?

YVONNE. Who make fun of you because you're bright.

LATISHA. My friends. Some of them are my friends.

YVONNE. Oh ... I ...

LATISHA. I mean, they don't mean to ...

YVONNE. They're not your real friends. I know what you're going through.

PAT and JEFF. *(To Yvonne.)* What did you talk about?

YVONNE. *(To Pat.)* Private matters.

YVONNE. *(To Jeff.)*	LATISHA. *(To Yvonne.)*
She thought ...	I thought ...

YVONNE. I grew up rich.

JEFF. *(To Yvonne.)* I thought you grew up rich too.

LATISHA. You remind me of the rich kids at my school.

YVONNE. *(To Jeff.)* We were very well off. *(To Latisha.)* No, I wasn't rich at all. *(To Jeff.)* But I didn't want Latisha to know that. I was afraid she would shut down. *(To Latisha.)* Borderline ghetto, my father used to call it.

LATISHA. I live in one of those neighborhoods. The first six blocks are great. The seventh is a shithole.

YVONNE. *(To Latisha.)* People made fun of me before I went to boarding school. Even my own sister. Oreo. Wonderbread. Black cracker. I heard it all. One time this kid, Jon-Jon, he sprayed white paint all over my face while we were on the school bus. I ran home crying, but my father wouldn't let me feel sorry for myself. He told me to scrub my face and go right back to school and I did.

LATISHA. God, I could never.

---

* *German language is very musical.*
  Call me if you would like to practice at all.
  Thank you, I will.

YVONNE. *(To Latisha.)* I was scared as hell, but my father told me I had to show them that I could not be stopped, could not be intimidated, and I tell you Latisha those ignorant niggers I went to school with never amounted to a damn thing. My sister got pregnant in the eighth grade by the same boy who sprayed paint on me. She called me a few years ago to ask me for money. I reminded her of that day on the bus. *(Pause.)* Then she was the one crying. *(To Pat and Jeff.)* I encouraged her. I made her feel her hard work would be rewarded.

PAT. *(To Yvonne.)* I have an appointment at three.

YVONNE. *(To Pat and Jeff.)* And suddenly, out of the blue, she tells me.

LATISHA. I'm in this gang.

NEIL. *(To Pat.)*	PAT. *(To Yvonne.)*
Oh, Lord.	Oh, Lord.

PAT. *(To Yvonne.)* Here we go. More pathology.

NEIL. *(To Pat.)*	PAT. *(To Yvonne.)*
What gang?	What gang?
YVONNE. *(To Latisha.)*	JEFF. *(To Yvonne.)*
What gang?	What gang?

LATISHA. The AOBs. We dress like guys and roll people.

YVONNE. Roll people?

LATISHA, PAT and JEFF. *(To Yvonne.)* That means rob.

YVONNE. *(To Pat.)* I know what it means. *(To Jeff.)* Latisha told me what it means.

LATISHA. We dress like brothers so we won't be ID'd, and rob Korean groceries and stuff, but no one ever catches us 'cause we look like any other brother on the street. That's where we got the name from. The AOBs. Any Other Brother. The po-po …

PAT. *(To Yvonne.)*	YVONNE. *(To Latisha.)*
The what?	The what?
JEFF. *(To Yvonne.)*	NEIL. *(To Pat.)*
The what?	The what?

YVONNE. *(To Jeff.)* You should have seen Pat's face when I explained it to her.

YVONNE. *(To Pat.)*	LATISHA. *(To Yvonne.)*
That means cop.	That means cop.

PAT. *(To Yvonne and Neil.)* Must be a recent slang.

YVONNE. *(To Pat.)* No, I don't think so.

LATISHA. The cops ain't looking for no girl so we don't get caught. *(Pause.)* Until now. Now, we kinda worried. Kinda in trouble.

YVONNE. *(To Latisha.)* Why?

LATISHA. Yo! You can't tell nobody. And I mean nobody.

YVONNE. *(To Latisha.)* No, no, I won't.

LATISHA. I'm telling you I'll jack you up for real.

YVONNE. *(To Latisha.)* I won't tell.

LATISHA. *(Pause.)* We capped that teacher.

PAT and JEFF. *(To Yvonne.)* What?

NEIL. *(To Pat.)* What?	YVONNE. *(To Latisha.)* What?
JEFF. *(To Yvonne.)* She said that?	NEIL. *(To Pat.)* She said that?

LATISHA. I ... I think ... I think ... my girl did it which is as good as me doing it 'cause we one. You know what I'm saying?

JEFF. Two seconds ago she was speaking ...

PAT. *(To Yvonne.)* Did she say that in Italian or German? Maybe Dutch.

YVONNE. *(To Pat and Jeff.)* She said it in English. She changed just like that. Got all street and hard. Then someone walked in and Latisha shut down. Became a young, scared girl. Before I left she came up to me and ...

LATISHA. Please, please don't tell anybody anything I told you.

YVONNE. I ...

LATISHA. No, please, you know, we got to talking and I got carried away. I shouldn't have said anything.

YVONNE. Latisha, you know I'm a reporter. *(Pause.)* I'm a reporter.

LATISHA. No! No! Listen, I was just talking to you. I mean you look kinda out of place here. Like me. Like I feel all the time. *(Yvonne tries to interrupt. Continuing.)* So I chatted you up but really. I ... Look, if you tell I will be in real trouble for real and I don't mean with my mother either. My girls will hurt me. Really hurt me.

YVONNE. Latisha ...

LATISHA. And kill me. I'm telling you. Just ... you can't say anything. Alright? Alright?

YVONNE. OK ... OK ...

JEFF. *(To Yvonne.)* What did Pat have to say.	NEIL. *(To Pat.)* What did you say?

PAT. Have you told anyone else?

YVONNE. No.

NEIL. *(To Pat.)* Anyone?

PAT. *(To Yvonne.)* The police?

YVONNE. No.

PAT. *(To Yvonne.)* Well, that's good. I think this story is about a sister succumbing to the image. Used to be just young brothers but now thanks to MTV and I'm ashamed to say, BET, we've got the gangster bitch to contend with ... This girl ... These girls have succumbed to the image.

JEFF. *(To Yvonne.)* What?! That's not the story.

NEIL. *(To Pat.)* What about my story?

YVONNE. *(To Jeff.)* I didn't think so either. *(To Pat.)* Listen, I don't know anything about all that.

PAT. *(To Neil.)* I don't know ...

YVONNE. *(To Pat.)* I mean I don't know why these girls are forming these gangs. I'm not examining the sociological ramifications because above all else this is a crime story.

NEIL. *(To Pat.)* What do you mean you don't know?

YVONNE. *(To Pat.)* A horrible crime has been committed.

JEFF. Good for you Yvonne.

NEIL. *(To Pat.)* That's fucked up.

YVONNE. Thank you. I laid into her, I did. *(To Pat self-righteously.)* We can talk about image and social responsibility later. It's a crime story.

PAT. *(To Yvonne.)* Uh-huh. *(To Neil.)* I have to follow up on this, Neil.

YVONNE. *(To Pat.)* Just a crime story.

PAT. We don't have the facts.

NEIL. *(To Pat.)* What about my research?

PAT. *(To Yvonne.)* We don't know the circumstances of this so-called murder.

NEIL. *(To Pat.)* I'm telling you those Dunns are not all they seem.

PAT. *(To Yvonne.)* That Dunn woman was half-Italian ...

JEFF. *(To Yvonne.)* Half-Italian?

PAT. *(To Yvonne.)* If these girls did commit these crimes ...

JEFF. She said that?

NEIL. Pat, just give me a chance ...

PAT. *(To Yvonne.)* I want to explore the circumstances.

NEIL. *(To Pat.)* ... to follow my leads.

YVONNE. *(To Pat.)* We're not a social service agency.

PAT. *(To Neil.)* I have to do this.

YVONNE. *(To Pat.)* It's a crime story first.

PAT. *(To Neil.)* I have to.

YVONNE. *(To Pat.)* Save analysis for later.

NEIL. *(To Pat.)* No.

YVONNE. *(To Pat.)* But it's a crime story now.

NEIL. *(To Pat.)* I'm writing my story.

YVONNE. *(To Pat.)* That's how I'm writing it.

PAT. *(To Yvonne and Neil.)* Not for me you're not.

JEFF. *(To Yvonne.)* You can write it for Metro.

YVONNE. *(To Jeff.)* I thought so.

NEIL. *(To Pat.)* Oh, no?

YVONNE. *(To Pat.)* Then I'll write it for someone else.

PAT. *(To Yvonne.)* Alright then …

NEIL. *(To Pat.)* Someone else will want my story.

PAT. *(To Yvonne.)* You can pursue your story. *(Pause.)* For Outlook. *(To Neil.)* I'm going to pursue Yvonne's story.

NEIL. *(To Pat.)* Well, goddamn.

YVONNE. *(To Pat.)* Excuse me?

NEIL. *(To Pat.)* You don't have to do anything you don't want to, Pat.

PAT. *(To Yvonne.)* Pursue your story. *(To Neil.)* I don't control the news.

YVONNE. *(To Pat.)* Thank you.

PAT. *(To Neil.)* We have a responsibility. You know that.

NEIL. *(To Pat.)* You wanted my story a week ago. You wanted it before uncertain sister arrived.

PAT. *(To Neil.)* Listen Neil … *(To Yvonne.)* But I'm going to have Neil cover this AOB story as well.

YVONNE. *(To Pat.)* What?

YVONNE. *(Continued, to Pat.)* You can't.	JEFF. *(To Yvonne.)* She can't.

PAT. I will.

NEIL. *(To Pat.)* Alright.

YVONNE. You have to transfer me, Jeff. You have to.

JEFF. I can't.

NEIL. *(To Pat.)* I'll do it.

Scene 5

Lights up on Jessica watching infomercial. Deeply depressed, she looks like she hasn't left the house or showered for days.

Scene 6

Lights up on Neil, Pat, Yvonne, Jeff.

YVONNE. *(To Jeff.)* I'm fine. I'm fine. But I don't trust Neil.

JEFF. *(To Yvonne.)* Don't worry about Neil.

PAT. *(To Neil.)* This is your story.

NEIL. *(To Pat.)* It's going to get ugly.

JEFF. *(To Yvonne.)* You can handle him.

JEFF. *(To Yvonne.)*	NEIL. *(To Pat.)*
You've got the upper hand.	She's got the advantage.
YVONNE. *(To Jeff.)*	PAT. *(To Neil.)*
I told Pat everything.	I told you everything she told me.

JEFF. *(To Yvonne.)* She doesn't know that.

NEIL. *(To Pat.)* How do you know she told you everything?

JEFF. *(To Yvonne.)* Neither does Neil.

PAT. *(To Neil.)* You're a good reporter.

JEFF. *(To Yvonne.)* You're a great reporter.

PAT. *(To Neil.)* Don't sell yourself short.

JEFF. *(To Yvonne.)* Remember that.

PAT. *(To Neil.)* We're counting on you.

JEFF. *(To Yvonne.)* Good luck, honey. *(Neil and Yvonne go to opposite sides of the stage. In center of stage are several characters. When characters are speaking on the telephone, spotlight goes on them. Scene begins with the sound of a phone ringing several times.)*

YVONNE. Hi, my name is Yvonne Robinson. I'm a reporter for *The Daily.*

NEIL. Neil Patterson. I work for *The Daily.*

YVONNE. I spoke to you last week at the community center.

NEIL. Sister, I was hoping you could help me out a bit. *(During the following the black woman speaks only to Yvonne.)*

BLACK WOMAN. You were supposed to interview me, but you didn't. *(During the following the black female speaks only to Neil.)*

BLACK FEMALE. What is it?

YVONNE. Yes, well. I apologize for that.

NEIL. The Northside Community Center?

YVONNE. I'd like to talk to you now.

25

NEIL. I understand you worked there.

BLACK WOMAN. I liked it.

BLACK FEMALE. It was a job. You know, paid the bills.

YVONNE and NEIL. Uh-huh.

YVONNE. And the girls. What was it like working with them?

NEIL. … mentoring the little sisters.

BLACK WOMAN. Like I said. I liked it.

BLACK FEMALE. It was alright. You know, alright.

YVONNE. You keep talking in the past tense. Did you quit your job?

NEIL. Can you be a little more specific … *(Trying a new approach — ghetto.)* Can you break that down for me, sister?

BLACK WOMAN. They closed the center this morning.

BLACK FEMALE. No notice or nothing. I got bills to pay. You know anybody hiring?

YVONNE. Closed? Just like that?

NEIL. Are you sure?

BLACK WOMAN. There was a note on the door. Closed.

BLACK FEMALE. I can type real good. They must need a typist at a newspaper.

BLACK WOMAN. I called and called …

YVONNE. *(To Jeff.)* … And called.

NEIL. *(To Pat.)* … Went by there.

YVONNE. *(To Jeff.)* Just a note on the door.

NEIL. *(To Pat.)* Closed.

PAT. *(To Neil.)* That's strange.

JEFF. *(To Yvonne.)* Weird. Really weird.

JEFF. *(Continued, to Yvonne.)*	NEIL. *(To Pat.)*
What school does	Do you know what school
Latisha go to?	Latisha goes to?

PAT. *(To Neil.)* She didn't say.

YVONNE. *(To Jeff.)* I didn't think to ask. It was just so fast.

PAT. *(To Neil.)* Yvonne said something about …

YVONNE. *(To Jeff.)* I know her parents grew up in Philly.

JEFF. *(To Yvonne.)* That's a lead?

NEIL. *(To Pat.)* Oh, OK. I'll call all the black people in Philly and ask them if they know a sister named Latisha.

YVONNE. *(To Jeff.)* I was just saying.

PAT. *(To Neil.)* You don't have to be a smart-ass. *(Pause.)* See if you can contact some of the other students from the center.

JEFF. *(To Yvonne.)* Maybe they have her home number.

PAT. *(To Neil.)* The students are who you should be talking to anyway. *(Sound of the phone ringing.)*

YVONNE. … *The* …

NEIL. … *Daily* …

YVONNE. … Few …

NEIL. … Questions …

YVONNE. I understand your daughter went …

NEIL. … To the after-school program … *(During the following the mother speaks only to Yvonne.)*

MOTHER. No, you're mistaken. *(During the following the female speaks only to Neil.)*

FEMALE. I guess she did. I don't know.

YVONNE. Isn't your daughter named …

NEIL. You don't know?

MOTHER. She goes to the program on the south side. It's less dangerous over there.

FEMALE. She ran up out of here about three weeks ago. I ain't seen her since.

YVONNE. How do you know that?

NEIL. Oh … I'm very sorry to have bothered you. I hope you … um … Sorry to have bothered you, sister. Goodbye.

MOTHER. My girlfriend's daughter goes there. Is that what you're writing about 'cause they've been closing down a lot of these shady community centers. *(Phone rings. During the following the assistant speaks only to Neil.)*

NEIL. Hello there sister. Listen, I was wondering if you could help me out a bit.

ASSISTANT. A listing of all our students named Latisha? Who is this again?

YVONNE. Ever heard of any gang activity at these centers?

NEIL. Well, sister, I'm sure someone as qualified as yourself can help me.

ASSISTANT. I don't think you're authorized to have that type of information. What's this about anyway?

MOTHER. What?! No! I can't speak for Northside though. I don't know anything about them.

ASSISTANT. Well, I can tell you we don't have any students named Latisha. I can tell you that.

NEIL. You sound familiar sister. Did you go to Howard? Are you a member of the Deltas? *(Yvonne dials number.)*

ASSISTANT. Come on brother, you trying to flirt. *(A phone rings.*

27

A woman answers.)

FRIEND. *(During the following she speaks only to Yvonne.)* Yes, my daughter went to the Northside Community Center.

ASSISTANT. You don't even know what I look like. *(Pause.)* What you look like?

FRIEND. She liked the program. She liked the other girls.

ASSISTANT. The AO what?

FRIEND. What's this story about anyway?

ASSISTANT. The AOBs? I have never heard of anything like that.

FRIEND. My daughter is not in a gang, and she doesn't know anything about gangs. Why don't you all ever write about something positive?

ASSISTANT. I'm sorry. I can't help you. I'm not a Delta. Goodbye.

NEIL. *(To Pat.)* I don't know …

YVONNE. *(To Jeff.)* I'm so tired.

NEIL. *(To Pat.)* Something is not right here. A girl like Latisha, speaks several languages, smart.

YVONNE. *(To Jeff.)* I should be able to transfer now. Not after the story.

PAT. *(To Neil.)* So what are you saying?

JEFF. *(To Yvonne.)* If you get the story they'll have to transfer you. If someone else gets it …

NEIL. *(To Pat.)* I've been asking around. Plenty of Latishas. No Latisha like that. A girl like that would stand out to somebody, even if she was trying to hide it.

PAT. *(To Neil.)* So what are you saying?

YVONNE. *(To Jeff.)* If someone else gets it?!

NEIL. *(To Pat.)* I don't know what I'm saying.

YVONNE. *(To Jeff.)* Don't play psychological games with me.

NEIL. *(To Pat.)* I think my original story about the wife is still valid.

YVONNE. I get enough of that shit from Pat and Neil.

JEFF. Yvonne, honey.

PAT. Neil …

JEFF and PAT. This story will make your career.

NEIL and YVONNE. Alright, alright.

YVONNE. *(To Jeff.)* I will find this girl.

NEIL. *(To Pat.)* I will get the story.

YVONNE. *(To Jeff.)*	NEIL. *(To Pat.)*
Wherever she is.	Whatever it is.

PAT. I'm sure you will.

JEFF. I have total confidence in you.

PAT. But I think you should try a different approach.

JEFF. We need to get a little more creative here.

PAT. Sister girl probably knows more than she let on.

JEFF. You know put together you two probably have opposite sides of a puzzle.

PAT. So use your extraordinary Howard U charm to …

JEFF. I think if you were nice to him, a little nicer, you could probably find out a lot.

NEIL. What do you mean?

YVONNE. What are you suggesting?

YVONNE.	NEIL.
Sleep with him?	Sleep with her?

JEFF and PAT. No!

JEFF. *(To Yvonne.)* God! What? Just have dinner or something.

PAT. *(To Neil.)* Why would you even go there? Just hang out with her casually, find out what you can.

JEFF. *(To Yvonne.)* It won't be that hard.

PAT. *(To Neil.)* It will be easy. *(Yvonne and Neil go to the middle of the stage.)*

JEFF. *(To Yvonne.)* Meet somewhere nice.

PAT. *(To Neil.)* That new place on Ivy is really nice.

JEFF. *(To Yvonne.)* Be polite.

PAT. *(To Neil.)* Hide your contempt.

NEIL. *(To Yvonne.)* Hello sister.

YVONNE. *(To Neil.)* Neil, I'm glad you could come.

PAT. *(To Neil.)* Dance around the topic.

JEFF. *(To Yvonne.)* Be sweet.

NEIL. *(To Pat.)* Uncertain sisters love it when you pay.

YVONNE. *(To Jeff.)* Black men like him love to show off by buying expensive dinners.

PAT. *(To Neil.)* See?

JEFF. *(To Yvonne.)* You know what you're doing.

NEIL. *(To Yvonne.)* Would you like some wine?

YVONNE. *(To Neil.)* Sure, whatever you recommend.

NEIL. *(To Yvonne.)* Oh, no. Please. You do it. Ripple was a delicacy in my house. *(To Pat.)* Uncertain sisters like it when you're humble. Show you're beneath them.

YVONNE. *(To Jeff.)* It will be good if I compliment him. *(To Neil.)* Listen, I was going through some of the story archives. I loved your story on … *(To Jeff.)* I'll have to find something.

NEIL. *(To Pat.)* I have to stay away from the hint of anything sexual. Uncertain sisters don't like flirting unless they're in control. Then, I'll make it seem like I'm on her side. *(To Yvonne.)* You know … I hate to say it, but Pat …

YVONNE. *(To Neil.)* What?

NEIL. *(To Yvonne.)* She's really been trying my nerves lately.

PAT. *(To Neil.)* That's good. Make me the common enemy.

YVONNE. *(To Jeff.)* I'll invoke the name of THE MAN. *(To Neil.)* I was really naive when I started work. I'm starting to sense a lot of racism. Subtle racism.

JEFF. Yeah, that's fine but don't mention my name and the word racism in the same sentence.

NEIL. *(To Yvonne.)* It's been frustrating. I really wish … I really wish …

YVONNE. *(To Neil.)* My own community makes me feel like a stranger. It's just a shame that …

NEIL. *(To Yvonne.)*	YVONNE. *(To Neil.)*
We should be working	We should be working
on this story together.	on this story together.

NEIL. *(To Pat.)* Then she'll tell me things because uncertain sisters love to give advice.

YVONNE. *(To Jeff.)* That's where he'll slip up, giving me advice.

NEIL. *(To Pat.)* Not a bad idea.

YVONNE. *(To Jeff.)* Not bad at all. *(Lights change. Yvonne and Neil introduce each other like they did at beginning of previous scene. Light change indicates time passing. Yvonne and Neil's body language indicate that things went very, very, very badly.)*

NEIL. *(To Pat.)* She was late.

YVONNE. *(To Jeff.)* I almost lost my nerve.

NEIL. *(To Pat.)* I started to leave.

YVONNE. *(To Jeff.)* He was pissed.

NEIL. *(To Yvonne.)* I thought you weren't coming.

YVONNE. *(To Neil.)* I got lost. Sorry.

NEIL. *(To Pat.)* That was a lie. I knew it.

YVONNE. *(To Jeff.)* I stayed in the parking lot for twenty minutes, trying to talk myself into it. It was a stupid idea. Stupid, stupid, stupid.

NEIL. *(To Pat.)* I remained cool. *(To Yvonne.)* Would you like a drink?

YVONNE. *(To Neil.)* No.

NEIL. *(To Yvonne.)* No? But you look hot …

PAT. *(To Neil.)* Uncertain sisters don't like the hint of anything sexual.

NEIL. *(To Yvonne.)* I mean … You're sweating pretty nastily over there.

YVONNE. *(To Neil.)* Well, it's hot in here.

JEFF. *(To Yvonne.)* Black men like him love to show off.

YVONNE. *(To Neil.)* Hey, listen. You know. I will have a drink.

NEIL. *(To Pat.)* Jekyll and Hyde this sister. *(To Yvonne.)* OK. What would you like?

YVONNE. *(To Neil.)* You pick.

NEIL. *(To Yvonne.)* OK. Well, let's see what we have here. The ninety-five white looks …

PAT. *(To Neil.)* Uncertain sisters love it when you're humble …

NEIL. *(To Pat — recalling earlier statement.)* … Show you're beneath them. Show you're beneath them. *(To Yvonne.)* Hey, what do I know. Ripple was a delicacy in my house. *(Dead silence from Yvonne. Continuing; to Pat.)* Bitch has absolutely no sense of humor.

YVONNE. *(To Jeff.)* Ripple? I haven't heard that joke since *Sanford and Son. (Awkward silence between them. Long pause.)* Oh … Oh … I read that story you wrote. I went through the archives and I read that story you wrote about the black firemen. It was … uh … brilliant.

NEIL. *(To Pat.)* I couldn't believe uncertain sister was trying to put one over on me. *(To Yvonne.)* It was alright.

YVONNE. No … no, better than that. I loved that you …

NEIL. It was alright.

YVONNE. Fine. *(Long awkward pause between them.)*

NEIL and YVONNE. So …

NEIL. How's the story coming?

YVONNE. What story? *(Yvonne and Neil both laugh awkwardly, fake.)*

PAT. Make it seem like …

NEIL. *(To himself. Recalling advice.)* … I'm on her side. *(To Yvonne.)* You know, I hate to say it but Pat …

YVONNE. Yes?

NEIL. Has really been trying my nerves lately.

YVONNE. Yeah, she's a real bitch.

JEFF. Yvonne, Jesus …

NEIL. *(To Pat.)* I wasn't expecting her to say that.

YVONNE. *(To Jeff.)* I wasn't even thinking. *(To Neil.)* I'm sorry. It just … I'm tired … I'm tired. *(To Neil and Jeff.)* It just slipped out.

JEFF. He'll slip up when he tries you give you advice.

YVONNE. *(To Neil.)* You know my own community makes me feel like a stranger.

NEIL. Yeah, well … When someone goes someplace for the first time that's how they usually feel. Like a stranger.

YVONNE. Did you write the book on blackness, 'cause I must have missed it.

NEIL. OK … Let's cut the bullshit.

YVONNE. Let's. You have no right to that story.

NEIL. What story?

YVONNE. That's real funny. You have no right to that story.

NEIL. I don't know of any story. I know of an alleged girl named Latisha and an alleged gang called the AOBs, but I have not seen anything even remotely resembling a story yet.

YVONNE. OK … OK … And how is that wife-mob connection story of yours holding up? Have you put the grand conspiracy together yet?

NEIL. I know what you came here to do!

YVONNE. I know what you came here to do!

NEIL. You're trying to bullshit me.

YVONNE. You're trying to bullshit me.

NEIL. Stop doing that. You can't even speak an original sentence.

YVONNE. No, you're the one who can't speak an original sentence.

NEIL. I know what you're trying to do.

YVONNE. I know what you're trying to do.

NEIL. You better stop that.

YVONNE. No, you better stop that. *(Neil and Yvonne storm off into areas where Jeff and Pat are.)*

NEIL. *(To Pat.)* Stupid …

YVONNE. *(To Jeff.)* Stupid …

YVONNE and NEIL. Stupid idea.

PAT. *(To Neil.)* If you were a better reporter …

JEFF. *(To Yvonne.)* … you wouldn't have to do this.

YVONNE and NEIL. Fuck you. *(They storm off. Then sound of a phone ringing. Yvonne picks up phone.)*

YVONNE. I'll talk with you tomorrow, Jeff. *(Lights on Latisha.)*

LATISHA. This is not Jeff. It's me, Latisha.

JEFF and YVONNE. Latisha!?

LATISHA. I heard you were looking for me.

YVONNE. Well, yeah.

JEFF. Yvonne, don't go.

LATISHA. Meet me at the Northside in one hour.

YVONNE. *(To Jeff.)* I have to go.

LATISHA. I'll give you the 411.

JEFF. No.

YVONNE. *(To Latisha.)* Alright.

JEFF. Let me go with you.

YVONNE. *(To Jeff.)* No, no, she said …

LATISHA. You best come alone too. I mean it.

JEFF. Don't be stupid. I'm going.

YVONNE. *(Continuing.)* I'm leaving now Jeff.

JEFF. Yvonne …

YVONNE. *(To Jeff.)* I'll call you later.

JEFF. Yvonne! Yvonne! *(She hangs up the phone. Jeff calls back. No answer. He runs out the door. After a moment there is the sound of the phone ringing. Then lights up on Neil and Pat. Pat and Neil speak only to each other unless otherwise indicated.)*

NEIL. *(Answering phone. Sleepy.)* Hello.

PAT. Neil …

NEIL. Pat, I'll talk to you tomorrow.

PAT. No, you won't … listen … *(Lights up on Yvonne and Jeff. Yvonne falls into Jeff's arms crying. Latisha speaks only to Yvonne.)*

JEFF. Shit, Yvonne. Where were you? I looked for you for two hours. I …

PAT. She got the story.

LATISHA. Did you come alone? I told you to come alone.

NEIL. What?

JEFF. What's wrong honey? What happened?

YVONNE. She's a baby.

PAT. She went right over my head to trust fund baby in Metro.

NEIL. She can't do that.

PAT. She did. They did.

YVONNE. Just a baby.

PAT. They didn't call me or anything, Neil. The night reporter in Metro, the brother with the gray hair just phoned me.

LATISHA. Listen, I heard you were looking for me and I have to tell you something.

PAT. Yvonne sent in a rough draft an hour ago.

NEIL. I'm not believing this.

JEFF. It's alright, honey.

PAT. Believe it.

JEFF. It's alright.

PAT. I have the draft right here. "Confessions of a Girl Gang Member," by Yvonne Robinson.

JEFF. Just tell me what happened.

NEIL. Read it to me.

PAT. *(Reading from copy.)* "In many ways she is like any other teenage girl around the country, concerned with boys, her hair and clothes."

YVONNE. *(To Jeff.)* She was scared and nervous. I asked her ... (To Latisha.) Is someone threatening you? Are you in ...

PAT. *(Reading from copy.)* "... But her sweet baby face and soft brown eyes hide a deeper truth."

LATISHA. Don't use my real name. Call me Sadeeka.

PAT. *(Reading from copy.)* "Sadeeka (not her real name) speaks several languages fluently. She is at the top of her class, and she is in a gang."

LATISHA. We don't wear no colors or nothing like that. No gang signs either. We lay low. We know who we are and we stick together.

PAT. *(Reading from copy.)* "Up until a few weeks ago, Sadeeka and her gang, the AOBs, committed what they considered to be petty crimes in the Northside area."

LATISHA. Don't nobody care when you rob black people. It don't make the news.

PAT. *(Reading from copy.)* "But then a Teach America teacher named Tim Dunn made a wrong turn."

LATISHA. I ain't mean to do it. He just looked like an easy mark.

PAT. *(Reading from copy.)* "And then Sadeeka's life changed forever."

LATISHA. You won't tell them who I am, will you?

YVONNE. *(To Latisha.)* No.

LATISHA. You promise? Because if you do ...

YVONNE. *(To Latisha.)* I promise you. *(Pause.)* I promise you.

PAT. *(Reading from copy.)* "Sadeeka killed Tim Dunn."

LATISHA. All those arrests and stuff. It's crazy. I can't sleep. I can't eat. I'm sick of it. I'm sick of this life.

JEFF. I'm calling my lawyer.

YVONNE. I know this is serious Jeff.

PAT. Hello, Neil? Are you there?

YVONNE. I know this could mean trouble.

NEIL. Yeah, I'm here.

JEFF. A lot of trouble.

PAT. Well?

YVONNE. But, you know, I'm not afraid.

NEIL. *(To Pat.)* Damn.

YVONNE. *(To Jeff.)* Because I got the story, Jeff.

NEIL. *(To Pat.)* Damn, damn, damn.

YVONNE. I got the story.

End of Act One

ACT TWO

Scene 1

Lights up on Jessica watching TV.

YVONNE. *(At a press conference.)* As a member of the human race, I feel for Ms. Dunn. I can't imagine her loss, but as a reporter I did my duty and those duties and responsibilities are protected by the First Amendment. Let the police investigate. It is their obligation to do so, but I won't reveal my sources under any circumstances.

TALKING HEAD 1. Well, I mean, as a black woman doesn't Miss Robinson have a responsibility to …

TALKING HEAD 2. Are you saying that black reporters should follow a different set of rules?

TALKING HEAD 1. Because the First Amendment doesn't have one set of rights for white reporters and one … *(Jessica switches channels. There is the sound of protesters chanting.)*

ACTIVIST 1. We are here to protest police brutality.

ACTIVIST 2. These sweeps ain't right.

ACTIVIST 3. My daughter can't do anything. She can't go to the store. She can't even go to school without being questioned by some cop.

ACTIVIST 1. I ain't seen so many cops here since Rodney King.

ACTIVIST 2. And this situation here ain't no Rodney King. *(Jessica switches channels quickly. After each sentence she switches the channel. Each sentence is spoken by a different voice.)*

VOICES. The First Amendment says … Tonight on News 12, girl gangs, where they live, how they live, and how you can protect yourself.

YVONNE. As a member of the human race, I feel for Ms. Dunn.

VOICES. Reporters aren't police officers … Nobody cares when black people get killed …

YVONNE. I can't imagine her loss.

VOICES. Tonight on News 9, Teach America teachers speak out

about the violence they face daily ...

YVONNE. But as a reporter, I did my duty. *(Jessica throws remote at screen, then lights up on Detective.)*

DETECTIVE. How are you feeling? *(Pause.)* How is everything with...? *(Points to Jessica's stomach. Indicating baby.)* My fourth grandchild was born just yesterday. Ten pounds, two ounces. A boy. *(Pause.)* You have to try and take care of yourself now. Especially now. I know it must be hard to ...

JESSICA. It's a girl.

DETECTIVE. Oh, really? That's wonderful. I ...

JESSICA. No, not that. The person who killed my husband was a girl.

DETECTIVE. Are you changing your statement?

JESSICA. It was a girl dressed like a boy. That's what the article said.

DETECTIVE. Yes, but ... Are you changing your statement?

JESSICA. Do I have to? *(The detective doesn't answer. Continuing.)* I want to change my statement. It was a girl. *(Pause.)* It was a girl.

DETECTIVE. Are you sure?

JESSICA. What difference does that make? *(Pause.)* Now, I hear they're wondering if maybe it was a student of Tim's seeking revenge or something. Did you hear that?

DETECTIVE. Yes.

JESSICA. But you know black kids don't really do that, do they? Black kids don't go into the cafeteria and shoot up everybody or stalk teachers and shoot them. Isn't that true? If one of Tim's black students was angry with him, the black student would have shot Tim right there in the moment. Isn't that right? *(Pause.)* Isn't that right? *(Detective doesn't answer. Continuing.)* Then we wouldn't be here. The black student would have been arrested and we wouldn't be here. *(Pause.)* A couple of months ago some people were even saying I had something to do with it. Like it was all some elaborate scheme I thought up. *(Pause.)* I don't know if it was a girl dressed like a guy or a guy dressed like a girl dressed like a guy. I only know the killer was black. *(Pause.)* The killer was black.

Scene 2

Lights up on Yvonne and Jeff reading letters.

YVONNE. Listen to this. *(Reading from letter.)* "Sellouts like you deserve to be lynched." *(To Jeff.)* A black person advocating lynching. How about that?

JEFF. How can you tell they're black?

YVONNE. The handwriting. Ghetto-like.

JEFF. Yvonne.

YVONNE. I'm just kidding.

JEFF. That's real funny, especially now.

YVONNE. Nobody's here but us. *(Pause.)* Did you read Pat's column? *(Lights up on Pat.)*

PAT. "Inner City Blues," by Pat Johnson. *(Pause.)* A few months ago I wrote an editorial about life lessons I had to teach my son. I sat him down and told him what it means to be a black man in America. I told him to keep his hands in the open when walking into a store. I told him to always say yes sir and no sir when addressing a police officer. I told him to expect the worst. *(Pause.)* I never imagined that one day I would have to tell my daughter the same thing.

YVONNE. She went after me again.

JEFF. I don't think it was about you. *(Pause.)* You know Pat's really angry about me taking that story. She sends like fifty memos a day about it. *(Jeff hands Yvonne memo.)*

YVONNE. You knew she would be. *(Yvonne reads memo.)* "Regarding 'Confessions of a Girl Gang Member' by Yvonne Robinson. Mr. Morgan's actions were not only a disrespectful violation of trust, they were a violation of newspaper policy. Miss Robinson is a rookie reporter still under probation. Since when is a rookie reporter allowed to break so many rules with so little consequence?"

JEFF. I really put myself out there for you.

YVONNE. I know you did. Pat would have destroyed that story. *(Pause.)* Anyway, like I was saying, the lawyer says if the police haven't done anything yet they probably won't do anything at all and, besides all that, I have First Amendment guarantees. She was really optimistic. *(Pause.)* I tried to tell Latisha that.

38

JEFF. You spoke to Latisha?

YVONNE. At home, about an hour ago. *(Noticing Jeff's expression.)* What's wrong?

JEFF. Nothing. *(Looking at letters.)* This one is short and sweet.

YVONNE. What does it say?

JEFF. "You're lying. I know you are."

Scene 3

Lights up on Pat and Yvonne at Pat's desk.

PAT. Congratulations.

YVONNE. Uh-huh. Thank you. *(Handing her papers.)* These are my transfer papers.

PAT. So, you're on your way huh?

YVONNE. They need your signature. *(Lights up on Neil and Jeff.)*

NEIL. *(To Pat.)* She could have let the intern handle that.

PAT. *(To Neil.)* I know. *(To Yvonne.)* I'd like to speak with you a minute.

YVONNE. *(Shoving papers at Pat.)* I'd really like to get over to Metro. Please send the papers over when you're done. *(Yvonne begins to walk away.)*

PAT. They're promoting you on one story, but your work here has been ...

YVONNE. Fine.

PAT. Sloppy.

YVONNE. It was fine.

PAT. You don't really believe that. *(Pause.)* The things you say and the way you say them matter because words matter. When I was going through hell integrating this paper that was the only thing that kept me going, knowing the power of words to effect change. You had an opportunity to do some great things at Outlook ...

YVONNE. If you hadn't given me such a hard time ...

PAT. If you liked me then you would have done your job? What kind of journalist do you want to be? *(Pause.)* You have to decide that. You can do a lot of good in Metro or you can do a lot of harm, but either way, every move you make reflects on us.

YVONNE. Us. Us who? You and Neil?

PAT. Us. Black people.

YVONNE. *(Pointing at transfer papers.)* Sign here and here. *(To Jeff.)* I think she knew they were coming. *(Two police enter.)*

POLICE. Yvonne Robinson?

PAT. *(To Neil.)* I had no idea.

POLICE. You're under arrest for obstruction of justice.

Scene 4

Lights up on Jeff and Yvonne in a car. Jeff is driving.

REPORTER. *(Voiceover on radio.)* In a precedent-setting motion, Judge Andrew Parker gave Metro reporter Yvonne Robinson forty-eight hours to reveal her source. If she fails to do so, Miss Robinson will be taken back into custody and incarcerated for an indefinite period of time.

YVONNE. No, left at that corner, left at that corner.

JEFF. Yvonne, just think, OK? Think. We have been driving around here for four hours.

YVONNE. It was dark Jeff. Very dark and I was scared.

JEFF. Yvonne, you have two days.

YVONNE. We stopped around here somewhere. It was around here.

JEFF. Just two days.

YVONNE. I'm looking! What do you think anyway? Latisha will just be hanging on the street corner pitching quarters?! *(Jeff turns a corner. Continuing.)* Where are you going?

JEFF. Home. Fuck this.

YVONNE. No, no wait. Jeff.

JEFF. I just don't understand.

YVONNE. Understand what? I told you it was dark. Latisha got into the car and told me to drive.

JEFF. Did you check your notes?

YVONNE. I couldn't take notes while I was driving.

JEFF. What about after?

YVONNE. After what?

JEFF. After you stopped. (Pause.) Just … just show me where you went.

YVONNE. I'm trying.

JEFF. OK … OK … You met her at the community center.

YVONNE. Yes.

JEFF. Latisha got in your car and told you to drive.

YVONNE. Yes.

JEFF. You drove for something like fifteen minutes then …

YVONNE. Went into an apartment.

JEFF. Whose apartment?

YVONNE. I told you already, Jeff. I don't know. Look around you. Do you see any street signs?

JEFF. You didn't think to ask where you were?

YVONNE. Latisha just started talking. I didn't want to interrupt her flow by asking her where we were at. (Pause.) It was run-down.

JEFF. Run-down? Really? In this neighborhood? How'd you get back then?

YVONNE. What?

JEFF. How'd you get back from wherever you were?

YVONNE. I don't know. I went towards something that looked like a ramp that led me back to civilization.

JEFF. Something that looked like a ramp. (Pause.) Aren't you scared?

YVONNE. Yes.

JEFF. I can't tell.

YVONNE. What do you want me to do? Cry?

JEFF. Why not? I have.

YVONNE. My father always said: Never let your enemies see you cry.

JEFF. I'm not your enemy. (Pause.) You cried that night.

YVONNE. What night?

JEFF. The night you saw Latisha. You fell into my arms crying.

YVONNE. Yeah.

JEFF. First time. Ever.

YVONNE. I wish it could be the last.

JEFF. I don't.

YVONNE. Why? Is the sex better when I cry?

JEFF. Goddamn it, Yvonne!

YVONNE. OK … OK … I'm sorry. I'm sorry. (Pause.) I should have gone straight to the National desk. I have the qualifications. If I were …

JEFF. What?

YVONNE. You know.

JEFF. Then say it.

YVONNE. No.

JEFF. Yvonne, do you have something you want to tell me?

YVONNE. Something like?

JEFF. I don't know ... Anything. *(Pause.)* You know no matter what you tell me ... *(Yvonne turns her head suddenly. She sees something out the car window. Continuing.)* What?

YVONNE. Nothing. I thought I saw ... *(Pause.)* For a second ... Let's go around the corner again.

JEFF. Two days, Yvonne. Two days.

Scene 5

Lights up on a black girl getting arrested by two cops. Yvonne watches arrest.

GIRL. Hey! Hey! I didn't do nothing. I didn't do nothing. Ask that reporter. Ain't she said who did it?

COP. No.

GIRL. Well, ask her.

COP. They will. Day after tomorrow.

GIRL. Day after...?! Ask her now.

COP. Come on.

GIRL. Ask her now. I ain't do nothing. I ain't do nothing. I ain't do nothing.

Scene 6

Neil and Pat enter on either side. During the following Neil and Pat only speak to each other and Yvonne and Jeff only speak to each other.

YVONNE. One day left. Twenty-four hours. Will you miss me when they take me to the big house?
PAT. What'd you find out?
NEIL. A lot.
YVONNE. *(Noticing Jeff.)* What's wrong?
JEFF. Nothing.
YVONNE. Why are you so ...
PAT. Well, tell me.
YVONNE. ... Sullen? I'm the one going to jail.
PAT. Tell me!
JEFF. I'm not, but ...
NEIL. Lie number one.
YVONNE. But what?
JEFF. I was thinking about that story.
NEIL. ... She told on TV a few days ago.
PAT and YVONNE. What story?
NEIL. You didn't hear?
JEFF. The story about your friend that was killed.
NEIL. At twelve or thirteen, I can't remember which, sister girl says she learned some harsh realities about race.
YVONNE. What about it?
NEIL. Her best friend was murdered.
YVONNE. I told you that story before.

| JEFF. | PAT. |
| No, you didn't. | Wait a minute. |

JEFF. Not that way.
PAT. Is this the story about some white friend who was killed and she didn't understand about death, let alone race, and she was shocked, just shocked to learn her friend was murdered by a black person and she had to learn forgiveness and grace and blah, blah, blah. She told that story in her interview. After that I was glad to leave.

JEFF.   NEIL.
You told me a different story.   She told a slightly different story.

JEFF. On TV, you said your friend was black and was killed by a white. You said …

NEIL. … At that moment she learned that race didn't matter because she knew that …

JEFF. … If your friend had been killed by a black person it would hurt just as bad.

PAT.   YVONNE.
Ha!   So?

JEFF.   NEIL.
You lied to me.   Story never happend.

YVONNE. I didn't.

NEIL. In black or white.

YVONNE. I made the story more interesting.

NEIL. I checked thoroughly. Yvonne has told that story seven or eight times, and each time the race of the victim has changed.

YVONNE. For the TV interviewer.

NEIL. One time the victim was Chinese.

YVONNE. More relevant.

NEIL. But the thing is this.

JEFF. Yvonne …

NEIL. I checked that exclusive little boarding school she went to. The one she loved …

JEFF. Did it even happen at all?

NEIL. And I came across an award-winning essay written by one of Yvonne's classmates.

YVONNE. What are you asking me?

NEIL. It was a very touching story about a murdered best friend and lessons learned.

JEFF. I'm asking you what I'm asking you.

NEIL. Never happened to Yvonne at all.

JEFF. Did it happen at all?

PAT. If she lied about that then …

YVONNE. What do you think Jeff?

NEIL. We should start an office pool. Will sister girl cave in?

YVONNE. What do you think?

PAT. Or will she get caught?

Scene 7

Lights up on Pat and Yvonne.

PAT. I need to speak with you a minute.

YVONNE. I'm on my way out.

PAT. Neil ran a background check on you. *(Pause.)* You never attended the Sorbonne. Never went to Harvard. Just UMass for two semesters before dropping out due to stress. I can't believe you got past Human Resources. When they hired me they checked everything, including my pee. When you walked into the room I guess they thought they hit the jackpot. You were living, breathing proof that black folks have and can make it to the promised land without bitterness, without blemish.

YVONNE. You want me to break down and cry?

PAT. I want to understand why you hate being black.

YVONNE. I don't hate being black. We have different definitions of the word.

PAT. I've never seen such self-hatred.

YVONNE. Oh, how nice for you. I didn't grow up in middle-class black utopia. Everybody singing songs and supporting each other. I got beat up for the very same things you got rewarded for.

PAT. That's your excuse? Bullies in the playground? Every black reporter is going to catch hell now.

YVONNE. Oh, well.

PAT. You're crazy. I guess you thought I would buy into your Latisha mess and when I didn't you circumvented me in an attempt to make me look weak and foolish, but when I expose you …

YVONNE. Complain and cajole, Pat. Maybe you'll get another section. Outlook 2. *(Pause.)* I have an appointment at three.

PAT. When you go down, you're not taking me … you're not taking Outlook with you.

Scene 8

Lights up on Yvonne alone, upset. Trying to compose herself.

YVONNE. *(To herself.)* She laughed at me. *(Lights up on Latisha.)*

LATISHA. Listen, I heard you were looking for me, and I have to tell you something. First off, my name is not Latisha, and I'm really, really sorry.

YVONNE. Sorry about what?

LATISHA. I'm not ... I'm not in a gang. *(Pause.)* And I don't know about any murder.

YVONNE. What? What the fuck are you talking about?

LATISHA. I was just playing with you. I was just playing.

YVONNE. Playing?! Are you kidding me? Playing?!

LATISHA. You know I just ... I go to boarding school and they are fascinated by a ghetto girl like me. Fascinated. How do you get your hair like that? Have you ever seen anybody murdered? I get so sick of it. So, you know, I just make up shit to pass the time. I tell them I'm in a gang, and my mother is on crack. They think I'm supposed to be like that so I just ... My mother is a librarian. I barely leave the house when I come home from school. *(Seeing Yvonne's expression.)* Are you ... Are you alright?

YVONNE. Why would you do this to me? Why would you? I told you about my sister, my life. I encouraged you. I helped you.

LATISHA. You helped me? No ... I ... See ... I ... *(Pause.)* Listen, I'm sorry. I'm ... *Mi dispiace.** *(Pause.)* I tell you it's hard keeping it real sometimes. *(Pause.)* I don't know ... *(Pause.)* When I saw you that day I wondered if it would work on one of us. I mean, I could tell you were different. Not really one of us. Like me kinda. Just the way you ... I don't know. *(Pause.)* I look around my neighborhood and I wish I could move. Everybody acts so stupid. But they're not stupid. They just act stupid. You know Frantz Fanon says the oppressed are taught to believe the worst about themselves. So I just wanted to see. I spoke Italian and German to you and you still believed I was in a gang. *(Pause.)* Just like the people at school. *(Pause.)* Just like them. *(Pause.)* So, you need to ...

* *I am sorry.*

46

YVONNE. I'm writing the story you told me. I'm writing about the AOBs.

LATISHA. There are no AOBs. There are no AOBs. I'll call the paper and tell. I'll …

YVONNE. You call the paper and I will tell the police that you killed Tim Dunn. You already told people at your school you are in a gang. No one will believe you. You fucking brat. This is my career. I will hurt you. I will.

LATISHA. This is crazy.

YVONNE. You laughed at me. Forget that Frantz Fanon bullshit, only a stupid-ass Oreo like me would fall for such a ridiculous story, right? You think you are the only one who has something to prove. It never ends, honey. It never ends.

LATISHA. I'm telling …

YVONNE. You think anyone will take your word over mine? They won't because keeping-it-real-wanna-be-gangster niggers like you make all black folks look guilty of something.

LATISHA. I'll … I'll jack you up for real … I'll … *(Yvonne laughs at her.)* I'll get somebody to … to … *(Pause.)* Please … please … I just … I was just playing!

YVONNE. You think it's funny all the white kids at school think you're in a gang? You think it's funny to be ignorant and crude? *(Latisha runs away.)* You want to keep keeping it real now? You want to keep — *(Pause to herself.)* — keeping it … *(Yvonne realizes she is alone. Phone rings lead us into the next scene.)*

Scene 9

Lights up on Neil, Pat, Jeff, Jessica, and Detective. Jessica and Detective only speak to each other.

JESSICA. *(Answering phone.)* Hello?

NEIL. *(To Pat.)* I've never seen a white man turn so white.

DETECTIVE. *(On phone.)* Jessica Dunn, please.

PAT. *(To Neil.)* What'd you say to him?

JESSICA. This is Jessica.

NEIL. *(To Pat.)* I said …

DETECTIVE. This is Detective Williams. I have some good news.

NEIL. *(To Jeff.)* Listen, I need to speak with Yvonne right now. Do you know where she is?

DETECTIVE. Miss Robinson is at the police station.

JESSICA. Excuse me?

DETECTIVE. I said …

JEFF. Yvonne is at the police station right now.

NEIL. *(To Jeff.)* Really?

DETECTIVE. Yes.

JESSICA. And?

NEIL. *(To Jeff.)* And what is she saying to the police?

DETECTIVE. She is going to ID the killer.

JESSICA. Thank you. *(Pause.)* Thank you. *(Lights up on Yvonne speaking with Detective.)*

YVONNE. Three weeks ago, about eleven P.M., I received a phone call from Sadeeka. She told me to meet her at the community center in the Northside area. I was alone.

NEIL. Wow. Giving up her source. Was that your suggestion?

JEFF. How can I help you, Neil?

NEIL. How long have you known Yvonne?

JEFF. About as long as you have.

NEIL. Really?

JEFF. Is there something you need, something I can …

NEIL. It just seems you two are pretty close.

JEFF. What is it, Neil?

NEIL. I'm just saying … I was looking for Latisha too you know.

JEFF. Yeah, I know.

NEIL. So, I'm just curious how she suddenly turned up at one in the morning. I mean, were you with Yvonne that night? Did you meet Latisha?

JEFF. OK. Let's just … Let's not play this reporter game, OK?

NEIL. OK.

JEFF. What is it?

NEIL. Well, I was going to go straight to Human Resources but I guess I'll tell you.

JEFF. Tell me what?

NEIL. I did a background check on Yvonne.

JEFF. What are you talking about?

NEIL. Her entire resume is a lie. *(To Pat.)* White boy was in total disbelief. You know, rumor has it he and sister girl are more than just friends. I almost feel sorry for her. I mean, it must be hard walking around pretending to be super-nigger all of the time. Most bourgie Negroes pretend that they're ghetto. She ghetto pretending to be bourgie. I was wrong. She's not an uncertain at all.

PAT. Don't you ever go over my head again, Neil. You understand me? Don't you ever do that again.

YVONNE. Just listen to me Jeff.

JEFF. Is your resume a lie?

YVONNE. Just listen.

JEFF. Neil told me. *(Pause.)* Neil. Do you know what that felt like to have Neil question me like that? You played me. From the beginning. You just … How could you do that to me, Yvonne?

YVONNE. I am who I was supposed to be. I was supposed to go on to the Sorbonne. I was supposed to graduate *summa cum laude.* I was supposed to have a master's degree in journalism.

JEFF. You were supposed to?

YVONNE. My father had expectations.

JEFF. So this is all your daddy's fault? You laugh at people who say things like that. Supposed to? Were you supposed to fuck me over too?

NEIL. Don't talk to me like a child.

PAT. Did you tell anybody else?

NEIL. No, what is wrong with you?

PAT. You just don't think, Neil. You don't think. I was going to have someone outside the paper call and inform management. I didn't want Outlook dragged into this mess.

NEIL. Trust fund baby printed that AOB bullshit not you.

PAT. They'll comb every single Outlook story for one error or typo and blame it on me. Me and Affirmative Action.

YVONNE. I fell apart.

JEFF. What does that mean? You don't fall apart. You don't even cry … You …

YVONNE. I did. All the time. For a while. I woke up one day and I couldn't stop crying. When I got better everyone I knew had graduated. Successfully. What they were supposed to be. So, I thought, easier to pretend than to explain. Just easier. *(Pause.)* You don't understand.

JEFF. No, I don't.

YVONNE. I didn't have a trust fund to fall back on. *(Pause.)* I grew up borderline ghetto.

JEFF. So? Did Pat have a trust fund? Did Neil?

YVONNE. I'm not talking about Pat and Neil. I'm talking about me. Four people. Two-room house. Government cheese and food stamps. All I ever wanted to do was get out.

JEFF. You crying poverty? I can't believe it. Poor little black girl Yvonne.

YVONNE. Shut up.

JEFF. Poor little welfare baby, gotta lie to The Man to get ahead.

YVONNE. Shut the fuck up. Poor little trust fund baby need a black girl on your arm to feel like somebody.

JEFF. I don't need you for anything.

YVONNE. Right. *(Pause.)* You could buy everything, except what I gave you.

JEFF. No, I could buy that too.

PAT. We have to keep quiet about this.

NEIL. Keep quiet? What good will that do? Trust fund baby has probably told by now anyway.

PAT. You said they're involved. He wouldn't risk revealing that.

NEIL. So call your friend or whoever was going to call management.

PAT. Then Jeff will know that the call came from us and he'll take Outlook down with him.

NEIL. This is crazy. She ain't O.J. She ain't even Michael. She's Clarence. Keep quiet? I just don't understand. Keep quiet. I won't.

PAT. You won't? You work for Outlook, Neil. *(Pause.)* You work for me.

YVONNE. That's accurate. You treated me like a whore. I never met your parents. You never asked to meet mine.

JEFF. Oh, OK. Let's drive over to the hood right now, and you can introduce me to Mr. and Mrs. ... Is Robinson even your real name?

YVONNE. Did you even tell your parents about us?

JEFF. Thank God I didn't.

YVONNE. The way you treated me at the office no one would believe we'd been dating. *(Pause.)* Unless I showed them the letters, notes and cards you've sent me.

JEFF. Oh, fuck. Are you blackmailing me or something?

YVONNE. No ... I'm just trying to show you that everybody has secrets. I have secrets. You have secrets. Latisha has secrets.

JEFF. There is no Latisha. There is no you. There is no Latisha. You think that you can still play me? You think that you can threaten me and I'll keep quiet? *(Long pause.)* I won't have to say anything, Yvonne. Pat and Neil will destroy you all by themselves.

NEIL. If we turn Yvonne in we can get to the bottom of this. We can get the community back on track.
PAT. What will the community be like when they take Outlook from us. All the work I ... we put in, gone. And I'm telling you they will take it from us. There will be some investigation. Internal. That's first. And then they'll give us some supervisor. It might even be a black person, a black Yvonne, but much worse, 'cause she'll be real. And then slowly but surely Outlook will be just like Metro. Nothing but black pathology and pain.

YVONNE. Maybe they won't.
JEFF. *(Laughing at Yvonne.)* Maybe they won't! You think Pat and Neil are going to link arms with you and march? I don't have to do anything. Say anything. Just step out of the way.
YVONNE. My father always said when trouble comes to our own we ... black people ... always, always close ranks.
JEFF. My father always said blacks are like crabs in a barrel. Dragging each other down.

NEIL. So, we'll fight for Outlook. You've done it before.
PAT. You weren't here before. I was. I know. *(Pause.)* Sister girl wasn't the only one to have a breakdown.

YVONNE. I will fight for my story. An innocent man was murdered and I found his killer. That's worth fighting for.
JEFF. It's over Yvonne. Just ... please. I'll go with you to the paper if you want. But you have to tell the truth about this. You have to. You made Latisha up, didn't you? *(Pause. No answer from Yvonne.)* Didn't you? If you tell ... *(Pause.)* Jesus, Yvonne, what did you say to the police?

NEIL. So we say nothing? Do nothing?
PAT. She will get caught eventually.
NEIL. Eventually. But in the meantime, there will be more arrests. In the meantime, the paper ... *(Pause.)* Oh, my God.
PAT. What? What's wrong?

NEIL. Oh, my God. Pat … I just … I just had a thought … I mean, what if…?

YVONNE. I told them the truth, Jeff. I told them the truth. *(Lights up on Detective.)*
DETECTIVE. *(To Yvonne.)* We'd like you to take a look at our lineup. *(Lights up on black girls in a lineup.)*
JEFF. *(To Yvonne.)* The police will check your story.
NEIL. *(To Pat.)* What if she…?
DETECTIVE. *(To Yvonne.)* Do you recognize anyone?
YVONNE. *(To Detective.)* Yes.
JEFF. *(To Yvonne.)* The cops won't just … They wouldn't just … *(Jeff realizes what she is saying.)*
DETECTIVE. *(To Yvonne.)* Are you sure? *(Yvonne points to someone in lineup.)*
YVONNE. *(To Detective.)* Her.
NEIL. *(To Pat.)* What will we do then?

End of Play

PROPERTY LIST

Handcuffs
Tissues (DETECTIVE)
Cell phone (PAT)
Memos (PAT)
Story (PAT)
Television with remote (JESSICA)
Menus (NEIL)
Letters (YVONNE, JEFF)
Memo (JEFF)
Papers (YVONNE)

SOUND EFFECTS

Classical music
Two gunshots
Police siren
Cell phone ring
Phone ringing
Television voices